Word

Confessions to Align with God's Will

Dr. Cheryl Kehl

Copyright © 2024 - Cheryl Kehl

All rights reserved. No part of this book may be used or reproduced by any means, graphic, electronic, or mechanical, including photocopying, recording, taping, or by any information storage retrieval system, without the written permission of the publisher and author except in the case of brief quotations embodied in critical articles and reviews.

Table of Contents

Introduction Unlocking the Power of Faith Confessions.......1
1. Abundance in All Areas of Life 4
2. Alignment with God's Timing 6
3. Boldness to Walk in Faith 8
4. Breakthrough in Difficult Situations................................10
5. Calling and Divine Purpose 12
6. Clarity in Decision Making..14
7. Compassion for Others 16
8. Confidence in God's Promises..18
9. Courage to Overcome Fear 20
10. Dedication to Spiritual Growth......................................22
11. Deliverance from Negative Thoughts 24
12. Discernment in Daily Life 26
13. Divine Favor in Relationships 28
14. Endurance through Trials..30
15. Faithfulness in All Circumstances 32
16. Family Harmony and Unity 34
17. Financial Stability and Provision...................................36
18. Forgiveness and Letting Go 38
19. Freedom from Past Hurts 40
20. Generosity and Giving Heart 42
21. Gratitude in Every Season 44
22. Guidance for Life's Path 46
23. Health and Healing 48

24. Hope for the Future 50
25. Humility and Servanthood 52
26. Integrity in Actions and Words 54
27. Joy in Everyday Life 56
28. Kindness and Compassion 58
29. Knowledge of God's Word 60
30. Lasting Peace of Mind 62
31. Love for God and Others 64
32. Mindset of Victory 66
33. New Beginnings and Fresh Starts 68
34. Obedience to God's Call 70
35. Open Doors of Opportunity 72
36. Patience in God's Process 74
37. Perseverance through Challenges 76
38. Protection from Harm 78
39. Provision for Every Need 80
40. Purposeful Living Daily 82
41. Renewed Strength and Energy 84
42. Restoration of Broken Relationships 86
43. Self-Control in All Situations 88
44. Spiritual Discernment and Wisdom 90
45. Steadfast Faith in Uncertain Times 92
46. Strength to Resist Temptation 94
47. Trust in God's Plan 96
48. Unity in the Body of Christ 98

49. Victory Over Adversity 100
50. Wisdom for Life's Choices 102

Introduction
Unlocking the Power of Faith Confessions

Words have immense power. The Bible teaches us that life and death are in the power of the tongue, and what we speak has the ability to shape our reality and influence our lives. Faith confessions are a unique way to harness this power intentionally, aligning our words with God's promises and purpose for us. Through faith confessions, we do more than just speak positive words; we declare God's truth over our lives, inviting His power and presence into every area we address. Words of Purpose: Confessions to Align with God's Will is designed to help you use these confessions as tools to unlock spiritual doors and walk in divine purpose.

Faith confessions are grounded in Scripture, rooted in God's promises, and spoken boldly to align our minds and hearts with His truth. When we make these declarations, we are actively choosing to reject doubt, fear, and negative thinking, replacing them with words that reflect God's vision for our lives. Each confession in this book is built around a central theme, covering aspects like purpose, victory, unity, and healing. They are designed to speak life, shift our perspectives, and strengthen our relationship with God.

Why do faith confessions work? Because they are an act of faith. Speaking God's promises is a way of activating our trust in Him, believing that His Word is true and powerful. When we declare these truths, we are not only reminding ourselves of God's faithfulness, but we are also inviting His presence into our circumstances. Faith confessions have a profound effect on our spiritual journey—they renew our minds, encourage our hearts, and increase our faith. They are a way of partnering with God, letting Him reshape our thoughts, emotions, and actions.

Faith confessions also unlock doors in the spiritual realm. They open us to divine possibilities, invite supernatural provision, and position us to receive God's blessings. By boldly declaring who we are in Christ, what God has done for us, and the promises He has made, we strengthen our faith and align ourselves with God's will. Each confession becomes an invitation for God to work, transforming us from the inside out and empowering us to live a life of purpose.

As you read through *Words of Purpose: Confessions to Align with God's Will*, approach each confession as a declaration of your faith and an opportunity to align yourself with God's heart. Speak these words with conviction, knowing that they have the power to bring about change. These confessions are tools, ready to unlock doors of blessing, healing, and transformation. As you declare each one, you are taking a step closer to the life God has designed for you, a life filled with His love, power, and purpose.

1. Abundance in All Areas of Life

Father, in the name of Jesus, I declare that I am living in abundance in every area of my life. I believe that You are a God of overflow, and I trust You to supply all my needs according to Your riches in glory. I thank You that my life is filled with Your blessings—physically, spiritually, financially, and emotionally. I align myself with Your promise of abundance, expecting Your favor to manifest in extraordinary ways.

I reject any mindset of lack or limitation, choosing instead to believe in Your limitless power to provide. I will not allow doubt or fear to rule my heart; instead, I stand firmly on Your Word that declares, "The Lord is my shepherd; I shall not want." I trust that as I seek You first, everything I need will be added to me.

I declare that I am a steward of Your blessings, using what I have for Your glory and for the good of others. I choose to be a giver, knowing that as I pour out, You will pour into my life abundantly. I open my heart and hands to receive from You, ready to see Your generosity overflow through me. My life will be a testimony of Your provision.

Thank You for the resources You are releasing to me, seen and unseen. I believe that You are arranging divine opportunities and connections that will lead to even greater abundance. I am patient and expectant, knowing that Your timing is perfect and Your ways are sure. I surrender my plans to You, trusting that You know exactly what I need.

Lord, I rejoice in Your goodness and faithfulness. I am confident that I will see Your hand of abundance in ways I have never imagined. I declare that my faith in Your provision grows stronger every day. I am grateful for every blessing, big and small, that You bring into my life. You are my source, and I praise You for the abundance You have in store for me.

In Jesus' name, Amen.

2. Alignment with God's Timing

Father, in the name of Jesus, I declare that my life is in perfect alignment with Your divine timing. I trust that You know the plans You have for me, and I surrender to Your schedule, knowing that it is for my highest good. I declare that I am not anxious about the future because I know that You hold every moment in Your hands. I rest in Your perfect timing, fully confident that You are orchestrating everything for my benefit.

I resist impatience and the desire to rush ahead. I will not be moved by what I see or by the expectations of others. Instead, I anchor myself in Your peace, trusting that Your timing is flawless. I am committed to waiting on You, understanding that You are preparing me for every blessing You have planned. I choose to be still and know that You are God.

I declare that I am aligned with Your will in every decision I make. I ask for Your wisdom and discernment to guide my steps, so I do not act outside of Your perfect timing. I believe that You are ordering my steps and opening doors at the exact moments they should be opened. I release any control, trusting that You know what is best for me.

Thank You, Lord, for the seasons of preparation and the process You are leading me through. I believe that every delay is purposeful, shaping me into the person You have called me to be. I know that You are using this time to refine and equip me for the future. My spirit is at rest, confident that You are faithful to complete the good work You have begun.

I declare that I will see the fruits of waiting on You. My heart is full of expectation, and my mind is at peace, knowing that Your timing is not only perfect but also abundant in blessings. I am ready to receive everything You have for me in the fullness of Your timing. I trust You completely and rejoice in the beauty of Your timing.

In Jesus' name, Amen.

3. Boldness to Walk in Faith

Father, in the name of Jesus, I declare that I walk in boldness, courageously following Your call on my life. I refuse to be held back by fear or doubt; I step forward in confidence, knowing that You are with me every step of the way. I believe that You have equipped me with the strength and wisdom needed to fulfill my purpose. Today, I choose to trust in Your power and move boldly in faith.

I reject the lies of insecurity and timidity, embracing the truth that You have not given me a spirit of fear but of power, love, and a sound mind. I declare that my faith is greater than any obstacle I may face. I choose to stand firm, unshaken by challenges, because I know that You are my foundation. My heart is rooted in the confidence that You are my strength.

I declare that my actions reflect my faith. I choose to speak words of life and walk in ways that honor You. I am not ashamed of my faith, and I am ready to shine Your light wherever I go. I believe that You will use my boldness to impact others and to bring glory to Your name. I am a vessel for Your power and a witness of Your goodness.

Thank You, Lord, for the courage to pursue my purpose without hesitation. I believe that as I move in faith, You are paving the way before me. I am not discouraged by setbacks, but I am strengthened by Your promises. I declare that my faith is growing, and my trust in You is unshakeable.

I praise You for the boldness that comes from knowing who I am in You. I rejoice that I am more than a conqueror, able to face anything because You are with me. I am confident in Your presence, declaring that nothing can separate me from Your love. My life is a testament to Your faithfulness, and I give You all the glory.

In Jesus' name, Amen.

4. Breakthrough in Difficult Situations

Father, in the name of Jesus, I declare that I am stepping into breakthrough in every difficult situation in my life. I know that You are a God who specializes in making the impossible possible, and I trust You to open doors that no one can shut. I stand on Your promises, believing that You are working behind the scenes for my good. I choose to lift my eyes above the challenges and focus on Your power and faithfulness. I am confident that breakthrough is coming, and I praise You in advance.

I reject any spirit of defeat or discouragement that tries to settle in my heart. I refuse to give in to doubt or fear, choosing instead to stand firm in my faith. I believe that every difficult situation I face is an opportunity for You to demonstrate Your strength. I know that You are bigger than any obstacle, and I trust You to bring me through victorious. I am anchored in Your promises, declaring that nothing is too hard for You.

I declare that I am filled with strength and resilience, empowered by Your Spirit to persevere. I know that You have given me everything I need to overcome, and I will not grow weary or lose heart. I am determined to press forward, keeping my eyes on You, the Author and Finisher of my faith. I trust that You are refining me through this season, preparing me for greater things. I am grateful for Your strength that sustains me.

Thank You, Lord, for the breakthroughs that are on the way. I believe that even now, You are making a way where there seems to be none. I declare that I am walking into a season of victory, a time where Your power is evident in every area of my life. I am filled with expectation, knowing that You are faithful to complete what You have started. My heart is full of hope, and I rejoice in what You are about to do.

I choose to speak life over every difficult situation, declaring that I will see the goodness of the Lord in the land of the living. I refuse to be discouraged, for I know that You are with me, fighting on my behalf. I declare that every setback is a setup for a comeback, a stepping stone to something greater. I align my words with Your promises, inviting Your power to work in my life. I am grateful for the hope and confidence that You have given me.

In Jesus' name, Amen.

5. Calling and Divine Purpose

Father, in the name of Jesus, I declare that I am walking confidently in my calling and divine purpose. I know that You have a unique plan for my life, and I am fully committed to fulfilling it. I reject any thoughts of inadequacy or uncertainty, knowing that You have equipped me for everything You have called me to do. I trust that You are guiding my steps and opening doors to fulfill Your purpose in me. I am excited about the future because I know that my life is in Your hands.

I declare that I am fully aligned with Your will, seeking Your guidance in every decision I make. I ask for wisdom and discernment to recognize the opportunities that align with my calling. I believe that You are positioning me in the right places, connecting me with the right people, and preparing me for every assignment. I choose to surrender my plans to You, trusting that Your ways are higher than mine. I am eager to see how You will use me for Your glory.

Thank You, Lord, for the gifts and talents You have placed within me. I commit to using them to serve others and bring glory to Your name. I reject any spirit of comparison, knowing that my purpose is uniquely mine, designed by You. I am content with who You made me to be, and I am excited to walk in the fullness of my calling. I know that as I use my gifts, You will multiply them.

I declare that I am a light in this world, positioned to make a difference wherever I go. I believe that every encounter, every opportunity, and every challenge is part of my divine purpose. I will not be swayed by distractions, but I will stay focused on what You have called me to do. I trust that You are directing my path and making my purpose clear. I am ready to make an impact for Your kingdom.

I speak life and purpose over every area of my life, declaring that I am on the path You have set for me. I refuse to let fear hold me back, knowing that You are with me. I am confident that I will fulfill the purpose You have designed for me, bringing glory to Your name. I rejoice in the journey, trusting that You are faithful to complete the work You have started in me. My heart is filled with purpose, and my life is dedicated to You.

In Jesus' name, Amen.

6. Clarity in Decision Making

Father, in the name of Jesus, I declare that I have clarity in every decision I make. I trust You to give me the wisdom I need to make choices that align with Your will. I refuse to be overwhelmed or confused, for I know that You are a God of order and direction. I believe that You are guiding my thoughts, aligning my desires with Your purpose. I am confident that I will make decisions that lead me closer to Your plan for my life.

I reject any spirit of confusion or doubt that tries to cloud my mind. I choose to seek Your face and listen for Your still, small voice. I believe that as I draw near to You, You will make my path clear. I will not be anxious about the future because I know that You hold it in Your hands. I am at peace, trusting that You are directing my steps.

Thank You, Lord, for the wisdom that is available to me through Your Spirit. I commit to walking in discernment, choosing what is right and pleasing in Your sight. I declare that my decisions are rooted in faith, not in fear or uncertainty. I ask that You sharpen my mind and make me sensitive to Your leading. I am grateful for the clarity and insight You provide.

I declare that I am led by Your Spirit, equipped to make decisions that reflect Your will. I am not swayed by outside influences or pressures; instead, I stand firm in my faith. I trust that You are giving me the ability to see beyond the surface, understanding the heart of every situation. I will wait on Your guidance, knowing that You reveal things in Your perfect timing. My decisions are aligned with Your purpose.

I choose to speak words of clarity and direction over my life, believing that You will lead me in the right way. I declare that confusion has no place in my mind, for I have the mind of Christ. I am confident that You are leading me into a season of clarity and purpose. I rejoice in the assurance that You will never leave me or lead me astray. My heart is filled with peace, and my mind is clear.

In Jesus' name, Amen.

7. Compassion for Others

Father, in the name of Jesus, I declare that my heart is filled with compassion for others. I thank You for the love and kindness You have shown me, and I ask for the grace to extend that same compassion to those around me. I recognize that every person I encounter is someone You love deeply, and I am committed to treating them with respect, empathy, and care. I open my heart to Your love, letting it flow through me to touch others in meaningful ways. I am grateful for the opportunity to reflect Your heart to those around me.

I reject any spirit of indifference or judgment that tries to take root in my heart. I choose to see people through Your eyes, understanding their worth and value as Your creation. I refuse to be hardened by the world's negativity, choosing instead to walk in love and compassion. I believe that as I show kindness, I am planting seeds of hope in the lives of others. My heart is open, and my actions reflect Your love.

Thank You, Lord, for softening my heart and giving me a spirit of empathy. I declare that I am quick to listen and slow to speak, allowing others to feel heard and valued. I am mindful of the struggles others face, and I am eager to be a source of comfort and encouragement. I trust that You will guide my words and actions to uplift and strengthen those in need. I rejoice in the privilege of being Your hands and feet.

I declare that compassion flows naturally from my life, impacting those around me. I am sensitive to the needs of others, ready to offer a helping hand whenever possible. I choose to invest in relationships, valuing people over possessions or achievements. I believe that as I show compassion, Your love becomes real and tangible to others. I am a vessel of Your kindness in a world that needs it.

I speak words of encouragement and life, choosing to uplift rather than tear down. I refuse to participate in gossip or negativity, aligning my words with Your heart for others. I declare that my speech is seasoned with grace, filled with kindness and understanding. I am committed to being a light, reflecting Your love in every interaction. My heart is set on making a positive impact.

In Jesus' name, Amen.

8. Confidence in God's Promises

Father, in the name of Jesus, I declare that my confidence is firmly rooted in Your promises. I believe that every word You have spoken over my life is true and will come to pass in Your perfect timing. I trust that You are faithful to fulfill every promise, and I stand on Your Word with unwavering confidence. I reject doubt and fear, choosing instead to believe that You are working all things for my good. My faith is strong, and my hope is anchored in You.

I reject any feelings of insecurity or uncertainty that try to creep into my heart. I declare that my identity is found in You, and I am confident in who You have called me to be. I will not be swayed by the opinions of others or by the challenges I face. I know that You are for me, and if You are for me, who can be against me? I am secure in Your promises, and I stand boldly in faith.

Thank You, Lord, for Your Word that gives me confidence and hope. I declare that Your promises are my foundation, a rock that I can stand on in every season. I am reminded daily of Your faithfulness, and I know that You are true to Your Word. I commit to spending time in Your Word, letting it strengthen and build my faith. I rejoice in the assurance that Your promises never fail.

I declare that I am expectant, ready to see Your promises manifest in my life. I choose to walk by faith and not by sight, trusting that You are orchestrating every detail according to Your purpose. I know that waiting on Your promises is not in vain, for You are faithful and true. I refuse to grow weary in the waiting, for I believe that everything You have spoken will come to pass. My heart is filled with hope and anticipation.

I speak words of faith, declaring that I am aligned with Your promises and purpose. I refuse to let doubt or fear steal my joy or confidence. I trust that You are working behind the scenes, arranging everything according to Your divine plan. I am grateful for the peace that comes from knowing Your promises are sure. My confidence is in You, and I rest in Your faithfulness.

In Jesus' name, Amen.

9. Courage to Overcome Fear

Father, in the name of Jesus, I declare that I am filled with courage to overcome every fear. I know that You have not given me a spirit of fear, but of power, love, and a sound mind. I trust in Your strength to help me face anything that comes my way, confident that You are with me. I choose to rise above fear, standing firm in the knowledge that You are my protector and guide. My heart is filled with peace, knowing that I am never alone.

I reject any thoughts of fear or anxiety that try to take hold of my mind. I declare that my mind is filled with peace, anchored in Your promises and truth. I will not allow fear to dictate my decisions or control my actions. I choose to trust in You, leaning on Your strength instead of my own understanding. I am free from the grip of fear, walking boldly in faith.

Thank You, Lord, for the courage that You have given me to face every challenge. I know that You are my strength and my shield, surrounding me with Your protection. I am grateful for Your presence, which gives me the confidence to move forward without hesitation. I believe that You are greater than any obstacle, and I trust You to guide me through. I am fearless, empowered by Your love.

I declare that I am bold and confident, ready to take on new opportunities and challenges. I am not afraid of failure, for I know that You are with me, and You work all things for my good. I am determined to live a life of faith, refusing to be held back by fear. I trust that You are leading me toward my purpose, and I am willing to take steps of faith. I am courageous, empowered by Your Spirit.

I choose to speak words of strength and faith, declaring that fear has no place in my life. I believe that as I align my words with Your promises, I am strengthened from within. I declare that I am victorious over fear, walking confidently in the path You have set before me. I rejoice in the freedom that comes from trusting in You. My heart is filled with peace, and my life reflects Your courage.

In Jesus' name, Amen.

10. Dedication to Spiritual Growth

Father, in the name of Jesus, I declare my unwavering dedication to spiritual growth. I commit myself to seeking You daily, drawing closer to Your presence, and allowing Your Spirit to transform me from the inside out. I know that spiritual growth requires intentionality, and I am willing to put in the time and effort to nurture my relationship with You. I reject complacency and choose to actively pursue the deeper things of God. My heart is set on growing in wisdom, knowledge, and understanding of Your Word.

I reject distractions that hinder my growth, choosing instead to prioritize my time with You above all else. I declare that I will not allow the busyness of life to pull me away from the path You have set before me. I will set aside time to read, meditate, and reflect on Your Word, letting it renew my mind and shape my actions. I am committed to removing anything that stands in the way of my spiritual progress. My focus is clear, and my heart is steadfast.

Thank You, Lord, for the tools You have given me to grow in faith, including Your Word, prayer, and the guidance of the Holy Spirit. I am grateful for the opportunity to learn, grow, and mature as I walk with You daily. I believe that as I apply Your Word to my life, I am being transformed into Your image. I am determined to grow stronger, wiser, and more resilient in my faith. My heart is open to Your leading and teaching.

I declare that my spirit is receptive to Your guidance, eager to learn and grow. I embrace correction and discipline, knowing that they are tools You use to shape my character. I am teachable, willing to listen to Your voice and follow wherever You lead. I trust that every experience, every lesson, and every challenge is working together to refine me. My life is a testimony of Your transforming power.

I choose to speak words of growth and maturity over my life, declaring that I am growing in faith, wisdom, and love. I believe that as I grow spiritually, I am better equipped to fulfill my purpose and serve others. I am committed to becoming all that You have created me to be, walking in strength and confidence. I rejoice in the journey of growth, knowing that You are faithful to complete the work You have started in me. My heart is set on becoming more like You each day.

In Jesus' name, Amen.

11. Deliverance from Negative Thoughts

Father, in the name of Jesus, I declare that I am delivered from all negative thoughts that try to invade my mind. I believe that You have given me the mind of Christ, filled with peace, hope, and positivity. I reject any thoughts of fear, doubt, or negativity that seek to steal my joy and peace. I choose to meditate on things that are true, noble, right, pure, lovely, and praiseworthy. My mind is a place of peace, and I declare that I am free from all negativity.

I reject any thought patterns that are contrary to Your Word, choosing instead to align my mind with Your truth. I will not entertain thoughts that bring fear or anxiety but will replace them with declarations of faith and confidence in You. I believe that You are renewing my mind each day, helping me to think thoughts that reflect Your love and goodness. I am committed to taking every thought captive and making it obedient to Christ. My mind is filled with peace and positivity.

Thank You, Lord, for the peace that surpasses all understanding, which guards my heart and mind. I am grateful for the power You have given me to overcome negativity and focus on Your promises. I declare that my thoughts are filled with hope, strength, and faith in Your power. I trust that as I meditate on Your Word, I am transformed from the inside out. My mind is a place of rest, anchored in Your truth.

I declare that I am vigilant in guarding my mind against negativity, choosing to dwell on thoughts that bring life and encouragement. I know that my thoughts shape my actions, and I am committed to thinking in ways that honor You. I will speak life over myself and others, filling the atmosphere with words of faith and love. I believe that as I cultivate positive thoughts, I am a light to those around me. My life is a reflection of Your joy and peace.

I choose to speak words of victory and freedom over my mind, declaring that I am free from every negative thought. I believe that I am more than a conqueror, able to overcome any mental stronghold through Your power. I refuse to allow negativity to control my thoughts or my actions. I am filled with peace, and I rejoice in the freedom that comes from having a mind set on You. My heart is full of joy, and my mind is a sanctuary of peace.

In Jesus' name, Amen.

12. Discernment in Daily Life

Father, in the name of Jesus, I declare that I am blessed with discernment in every area of my life. I trust You to guide me and help me make wise choices that align with Your will. I ask for clarity and insight, so I can see situations and people as You see them. I know that discernment is a gift from You, and I am eager to use it to navigate my daily life. My heart is open to Your leading, and I am confident in Your guidance.

I reject confusion and indecision, choosing instead to rely on Your wisdom. I will not be swayed by appearances or pressured by outside influences but will stand firm in the discernment You provide. I am committed to seeking Your guidance in every decision, trusting that You know what is best for me. I declare that my steps are ordered by You, and I am walking in Your perfect will. My spirit is attuned to Your voice.

Thank You, Lord, for the wisdom and discernment You provide through Your Spirit. I am grateful for Your guidance that helps me avoid pitfalls and make choices that honor You. I believe that as I seek You, You reveal the truth in every situation. I am filled with confidence, knowing that You are leading me down paths of righteousness. My life reflects the wisdom that comes from being connected to You.

I declare that my mind and spirit are sharp, discerning truth from deception. I am not easily influenced or misled because I have the mind of Christ. I choose to be cautious and thoughtful, seeking Your perspective in all things. I trust that You will give me clarity and insight, helping me navigate complex situations with grace. I am anchored in Your truth, and my decisions reflect Your wisdom.

I choose to speak words of wisdom and discernment, declaring that I am equipped to handle whatever comes my way. I am confident that You are leading me and that I will make choices that align with Your will. I declare that I am sensitive to Your Spirit, quick to recognize Your promptings. I am grateful for the peace and assurance that comes from knowing I am guided by You. My life is a testimony of Your wisdom and guidance.

In Jesus' name, Amen.

13. Divine Favor in Relationships

Father, in the name of Jesus, I declare that I walk in divine favor in every relationship in my life. I believe that You have positioned the right people around me to help me grow, encourage me, and strengthen my faith. I am grateful for the friends, family, and mentors You have blessed me with, and I trust that You are bringing even more positive influences into my life. I declare that every relationship in my life is blessed, filled with peace, love, and mutual respect. I am surrounded by people who uplift me and bring out the best in me.

I reject any spirit of division, misunderstanding, or strife that tries to come between me and others. I refuse to let negativity or conflict disrupt the unity and harmony You have established in my relationships. I declare that I am a peacemaker, walking in love and forgiveness toward everyone I meet. I trust that You are healing and restoring any broken relationships according to Your will. I am committed to being a source of love and encouragement to those around me.

Thank You, Lord, for the favor You have given me in every relationship, both personal and professional. I am grateful for the opportunities to connect with others, to learn, grow, and build meaningful bonds. I believe that as I walk in kindness and integrity, You will continue to bless my interactions and connections. I trust that You are guiding me to people who will help me fulfill my purpose. I rejoice in the favor that surrounds me.

I declare that I am intentional about building and nurturing healthy relationships. I am quick to listen, slow to speak, and eager to show love and understanding. I believe that as I sow seeds of kindness and respect, I will reap a harvest of strong, lasting connections. I am a vessel of Your love, bringing peace and joy to every relationship. I am committed to honoring You in all my interactions.

I choose to speak words of life and favor over my relationships, declaring that they are blessed by Your hand. I believe that You are connecting me with people who align with my values and goals. I trust that every relationship is part of Your divine plan for my life, and I am grateful for the people You have placed in my path. I am confident that I will continue to walk in divine favor, and my relationships will flourish. My heart is full of gratitude for the gift of connection.

In Jesus' name, Amen.

14. Endurance through Trials

Father, in the name of Jesus, I declare that I am filled with endurance to face any trials that come my way. I believe that You are my strength and my shield, sustaining me through every challenge. I trust that You are using every trial to refine and strengthen my faith, making me more like You. I am committed to persevering, knowing that Your grace is sufficient for me in all circumstances. My heart is steadfast, anchored in Your promises.

I reject any thoughts of giving up or giving in to despair. I refuse to be discouraged or defeated by the trials I face, for I know that You are with me. I declare that I am more than a conqueror, equipped to overcome every obstacle through Your power. I choose to keep my eyes on You, trusting that You are leading me through to victory. My faith is unshaken, and my spirit is resilient.

Thank You, Lord, for the strength and endurance You have placed within me. I am grateful for Your presence that gives me courage to keep going, even when the road is difficult. I believe that as I lean on You, I will find renewed strength each day. I trust that every trial is working together for my good, shaping me into the person You have called me to be. My spirit is filled with hope, and my heart is at peace.

I declare that I will not be weary in well-doing, for I know that in due season I will reap if I do not give up. I am committed to staying faithful, holding on to Your promises with unwavering confidence. I believe that every step I take is bringing me closer to the breakthrough You have in store for me. I will not let temporary trials steal my joy or my hope. My focus is on You, and I am determined to endure.

I choose to speak words of strength and perseverance over my life, declaring that I am equipped to handle whatever comes my way. I trust that You are developing my character and refining my faith through each trial. I rejoice in the knowledge that my endurance is producing a harvest of righteousness and peace. I am grateful for the growth and maturity that comes from trusting You in all things. My heart is full of courage, and my life reflects Your strength.

In Jesus' name, Amen.

15. Faithfulness in All Circumstances

Father, in the name of Jesus, I declare that I am faithful to You in every circumstance, no matter what I face. I am committed to serving You wholeheartedly, knowing that You are with me in every season of life. I trust that You see my heart and that You are pleased with my dedication to following Your ways. I choose to remain steadfast, honoring You with my actions, words, and thoughts. My faithfulness to You is unwavering.

I reject any spirit of inconsistency or compromise that tries to pull me away from my commitment to You. I refuse to let temporary challenges or distractions weaken my resolve to serve You faithfully. I declare that my loyalty is to You alone, and I will not waver in my devotion. I am grounded in my faith, unshaken by external circumstances. My heart is fixed on You, and I am determined to stay true to Your Word.

Thank You, Lord, for Your faithfulness that inspires me to be faithful in return. I am grateful for Your unchanging love and the security I find in You. I believe that as I remain faithful, You will reward me with Your blessings and favor. I trust that my commitment to You is strengthening my relationship with You, bringing me closer to Your heart. I rejoice in the assurance that You are with me always.

I declare that I am diligent in seeking You, setting aside time each day to connect with You. I am committed to growing in my relationship with You, building a foundation of trust and intimacy. I believe that as I prioritize my time with You, my faithfulness will flourish. I choose to stay focused on what truly matters, investing in my walk with You. My devotion is steadfast, and my life is a reflection of my love for You.

I choose to speak words of faithfulness over my life, declaring that I am dependable and consistent in my walk with You. I trust that as I remain faithful, You will guide me and open doors of opportunity. I am confident that my loyalty to You will lead to blessings beyond my imagination. I am grateful for the strength and courage to remain faithful, regardless of the circumstances. My heart is devoted to You, and my faithfulness is unwavering.

In Jesus' name, Amen.

16. Family Harmony and Unity

Father, in the name of Jesus, I declare that my family is blessed with harmony and unity. I believe that You are at the center of our home, bringing us together in love and understanding. I declare that peace fills our relationships, and that every member of my family is surrounded by Your love and grace. I trust that You are strengthening our bonds and aligning our hearts with Your will. I am grateful for the blessing of family, and I commit to nurturing our unity.

I reject any spirit of division, discord, or strife that tries to disrupt our home. I refuse to let misunderstandings or conflicts create distance between us. I believe that You are giving us the grace to communicate effectively and to forgive quickly. I declare that we are patient, kind, and understanding with one another, choosing to focus on what unites us. Our family is a sanctuary of peace and love.

Thank You, Lord, for the gift of family and for the love that binds us together. I am grateful for every opportunity to show kindness, compassion, and understanding to my loved ones. I believe that as we honor You in our relationships, You will continue to bless our home. I trust that You are using each of us to support and uplift one another. I rejoice in the unity and harmony that fills our lives.

I declare that I am a peacemaker in my family, committed to creating an atmosphere of love and respect. I choose to lead by example, showing patience, empathy, and kindness in all my interactions. I believe that as I sow seeds of peace, our family will grow stronger and closer. I am dedicated to building a home that reflects Your love and grace. Our family is a testament to Your goodness.

I speak words of blessing and unity over my family, declaring that our home is filled with joy, laughter, and understanding. I believe that You are protecting us from any harm or division, covering us with Your peace. I trust that every member of my family is guided by Your wisdom and surrounded by Your love. I am grateful for the harmony that You have established among us. My heart is full of gratitude for the unity in our home.

In Jesus' name, Amen.

17. Financial Stability and Provision

Father, in the name of Jesus, I declare that I walk in financial stability and provision. I trust that You are my provider, supplying all my needs according to Your riches in glory. I believe that You care about every detail of my life, including my financial well-being. I am grateful for the resources You have given me, and I commit to managing them with wisdom and integrity. I am confident that as I honor You with my finances, You will continue to bless and provide for me.

I reject any spirit of lack or poverty, choosing instead to believe in Your abundance and generosity. I refuse to be anxious or fearful about money, trusting that You are faithful to provide for every need. I declare that I am free from financial worries, knowing that my security comes from You alone. I choose to live with a mindset of abundance, confident in Your provision. My trust is in You, not in worldly wealth.

Thank You, Lord, for the blessings and opportunities You have placed in my life. I am grateful for the wisdom You provide to manage my finances in a way that honors You. I believe that as I am faithful with what I have, You will entrust me with more. I commit to using my resources to bless others and to further Your kingdom. I rejoice in the stability and peace that come from trusting in You.

I declare that I am a good steward of all that You have given me. I choose to be disciplined, wise, and generous with my finances, knowing that everything I have is a gift from You. I trust that as I give, it will be given back to me, pressed down, shaken together, and running over. I am committed to living a life of generosity, confident that You are my source. I am blessed to be a blessing.

I speak words of abundance and provision over my life, declaring that I lack nothing because You are my provider. I believe that You are opening doors of opportunity and leading me to new avenues of blessing. I am grateful for the peace and security that come from knowing You are in control of my finances. My heart is filled with faith, and my life reflects Your provision. I am confident in Your faithfulness.

In Jesus' name, Amen.

18. Forgiveness and Letting Go

Father, in the name of Jesus, I declare that I am free from the burden of unforgiveness, choosing instead to walk in grace and mercy. I believe that forgiveness is a gift from You, and I choose to extend it to others as You have freely given it to me. I release any resentment, bitterness, or anger that I may hold in my heart. I am committed to letting go of past hurts and moving forward in freedom. My heart is filled with peace as I embrace forgiveness.

I reject any spirit of unforgiveness or bitterness that tries to take root in my heart. I refuse to let past wounds control my present or dictate my future. I declare that I am empowered by Your Spirit to forgive fully and completely, holding nothing back. I choose to see others through Your eyes, with compassion and understanding. My heart is open, and I am free from the weight of unforgiveness.

Thank You, Lord, for the forgiveness You have given me, and for the freedom that comes with it. I am grateful for the grace that allows me to forgive others and to release any pain or hurt I may carry. I believe that as I forgive, I am healed and restored, walking in the fullness of Your love. I trust that You are working in my heart, teaching me to forgive as You have forgiven me. My spirit is at peace, and my heart is free.

I declare that I am a vessel of forgiveness, extending grace to those who have wronged me. I choose to walk in love and understanding, knowing that forgiveness is a powerful act of faith. I believe that as I forgive, I am making room for Your healing and blessings in my life. I am committed to letting go of the past and embracing the future You have for me. My life reflects Your love and forgiveness.

I speak words of peace and freedom over my life, declaring that I am free from any chains of unforgiveness. I believe that as I let go of the past, I am stepping into a new season of healing and growth. I am grateful for the joy that comes from walking in forgiveness and releasing all bitterness. My heart is light, my spirit is free, and my life is filled with peace. I rejoice in the freedom of forgiveness.

In Jesus' name, Amen.

19. Freedom from Past Hurts

Father, in the name of Jesus, I declare that I am free from the pain and limitations of my past. I believe that You have set me free from every hurt, every disappointment, and every wound that has weighed me down. I choose to release all burdens from my past, allowing Your healing power to restore my heart and mind. I am no longer bound by the experiences that once held me captive. I am stepping into a new season of peace, joy, and wholeness.

I reject any feelings of bitterness, anger, or regret that try to creep into my heart. I refuse to let past hurts define who I am or limit what I can become in You. I declare that I am free to move forward, unencumbered by the pain of yesterday. I am no longer looking back; instead, I am focused on the bright future You have for me. My heart is healed, and my spirit is renewed.

Thank You, Lord, for the healing and freedom that only You can provide. I am grateful for the strength to let go of the past and to embrace the new life You have given me. I believe that as I surrender my hurts to You, You are transforming my pain into purpose. I trust that You are using every experience to shape me into the person You created me to be. My heart is full of gratitude for the freedom I now have.

I declare that I am strong, resilient, and filled with hope, ready to pursue the life You have planned for me. I believe that every wound has been healed, and every scar is a testimony of Your power and love. I am determined to live fully, embracing each day with confidence and joy. I trust that You are guiding me forward, step by step, into a life of purpose and abundance. My past no longer holds me, for I am free in You.

I choose to speak words of healing and freedom over my life, declaring that I am whole and restored. I believe that as I walk in this new freedom, I am able to inspire and encourage others. I am no longer bound by fear or hesitation, but I am stepping boldly into the future. My heart is open to all that You have for me, and I am ready to live in the fullness of Your blessings. I rejoice in the freedom and healing that are mine in You.

In Jesus' name, Amen.

20. Generosity and Giving Heart

Father, in the name of Jesus, I declare that I have a generous and giving heart, just as You have shown generosity to me. I believe that everything I have is a gift from You, and I am committed to using my resources to bless others. I choose to be a cheerful giver, finding joy in helping those in need and supporting Your kingdom work. I know that as I give, You will continue to provide for me abundantly. My heart is open to give freely, without hesitation or reservation.

I reject any spirit of selfishness, greed, or fear that tries to hold me back from giving. I refuse to let the desire for worldly possessions or wealth keep me from being a blessing to others. I declare that I am not attached to material things, but I am focused on storing up treasures in heaven. I am content with what I have, trusting that You will supply all my needs. My joy comes from serving and giving, not from accumulating.

Thank You, Lord, for the resources You have entrusted to me and for the privilege of being a blessing to others. I am grateful for every opportunity to give, whether in time, money, or kindness. I believe that as I give, I am sowing seeds of love, compassion, and generosity that will impact others for Your glory. I trust that You are using my gifts to make a difference in the world. My heart is filled with gratitude for the joy of giving.

I declare that my giving is a reflection of my faith, an act of worship that honors You. I choose to be mindful of the needs around me, ready to respond with compassion and generosity. I believe that as I give, I am planting seeds that will bring forth a harvest of blessings. I am committed to being a faithful steward, using what I have to advance Your kingdom and serve others. My life is a testimony of Your provision and love.

I choose to speak words of generosity and abundance over my life, declaring that I am a vessel of Your blessings. I believe that as I give, You are multiplying my resources, allowing me to bless even more people. I am confident that my generosity is making a positive impact and bringing glory to Your name. I am thankful for the privilege of giving, and I rejoice in the blessings that flow from a generous heart. My heart is full, and my hands are open to share.

In Jesus' name, Amen.

21. Gratitude in Every Season

Father, in the name of Jesus, I declare that I am filled with gratitude in every season of my life. I thank You for Your faithfulness, for the blessings I see, and for those that are yet to come. I choose to focus on the good, to find joy in each day, and to appreciate every moment You give me. I know that gratitude opens the door to Your presence and fills my heart with peace and contentment. I am grateful for all that You have done, and I rejoice in Your goodness.

I reject any spirit of complaining, dissatisfaction, or entitlement that tries to take root in my heart. I refuse to dwell on what I lack or what has gone wrong; instead, I choose to celebrate the blessings You have given me. I believe that gratitude is a choice, and I am committed to expressing thanks in every circumstance. I will not let temporary setbacks steal my joy, for I know that You are always working for my good. My heart is at peace, filled with gratitude.

Thank You, Lord, for the countless blessings You have poured into my life, both seen and unseen. I am grateful for the love, peace, and joy that come from knowing You. I believe that as I focus on gratitude, I am opening myself up to receive even more of Your goodness. I trust that You are using every season, every moment, to shape me and draw me closer to You. My spirit is lifted, and my heart is overflowing with thanks.

I declare that I am a person of gratitude, quick to recognize and appreciate the blessings around me. I am committed to being a source of encouragement, sharing my joy with others and lifting them up. I believe that as I live in gratitude, I am a light in the world, a reflection of Your love and goodness. I choose to count my blessings daily, acknowledging Your presence in every part of my life. My heart is filled with joy, and my life is a testimony of Your faithfulness.

I choose to speak words of gratitude and thanksgiving over my life, declaring that I am grateful for every gift, every lesson, and every opportunity. I believe that as I cultivate a heart of gratitude, I am experiencing greater peace and joy. I am content with what I have, knowing that You are my provider and my source of all good things. I rejoice in the beauty of each day, confident in Your love and provision. My heart is full, and my life reflects Your goodness.

In Jesus' name, Amen.

22. Guidance for Life's Path

Father, in the name of Jesus, I declare that I am guided by Your wisdom in every decision and step I take. I trust that You have a perfect plan for my life, and I am committed to following Your lead. I believe that as I seek You, You will reveal the path that leads to my purpose and fulfillment. I am grateful for Your guidance, which provides clarity and direction when I need it most. My heart is at peace, knowing that I am never alone on this journey.

I reject any spirit of confusion or hesitation that tries to cloud my mind. I refuse to let fear or uncertainty keep me from stepping into the future You have prepared for me. I declare that my mind is clear, and my spirit is attuned to Your voice. I trust that as I draw near to You, You will illuminate my path and help me discern the right way. I am confident in Your guidance, and I rest in Your promises.

Thank You, Lord, for the wisdom and insight You give me as I navigate my life's path. I am grateful for the peace that comes from knowing I can rely on You in every season and circumstance. I believe that as I seek Your face, You will give me the understanding I need to make wise choices. I trust that You are leading me step by step, and I am willing to follow wherever You go. My life is anchored in Your guidance.

I declare that I am receptive to Your leading, willing to go wherever You direct me. I am sensitive to the promptings of the Holy Spirit, quick to respond to Your voice. I believe that every step I take is ordered by You, and I am ready to walk in faith. I am committed to aligning my decisions with Your will, allowing Your wisdom to shape my path. My heart is open, and my spirit is willing.

I choose to speak words of direction and purpose over my life, declaring that I am walking confidently in the path You have set before me. I believe that You are opening doors of opportunity and closing doors that do not align with Your purpose. I am grateful for the assurance that comes from knowing my steps are guided by You. I rejoice in the journey, trusting that every step brings me closer to the destiny You have designed for me. My heart is full of hope, and my future is bright in Your hands.

In Jesus' name, Amen.

23. Health and Healing

Father, in the name of Jesus, I declare that I am walking in health, strength, and divine healing. I believe that You are the God who heals, and I trust in Your power to restore every part of my body. I know that sickness and disease have no authority over me, for I am covered by the blood of Jesus. I choose to speak life, strength, and vitality over my body, declaring that I am healed in Jesus' name. My health is a reflection of Your love and care for me.

I reject any spirit of fear, illness, or infirmity that tries to take hold of my life. I refuse to accept sickness as part of my identity, for I am a child of God, created to live in health and wholeness. I declare that my body is strong, resilient, and filled with the power of God. I trust that every cell, organ, and system in my body is functioning as You intended. My faith is in You, my Healer, and I stand on Your promises.

Thank You, Lord, for the gift of healing and for the health You have given me. I am grateful for every day that I am able to live fully, enjoying the strength and vitality that come from You. I believe that as I continue to walk in faith, You will sustain me and keep me in perfect health. I am committed to taking care of my body, knowing that it is a temple of Your Spirit. My heart is filled with gratitude for the gift of life.

I declare that I am proactive in maintaining my health, choosing habits that support the strength and vitality You have given me. I believe that as I make wise choices, I am honoring the body You have entrusted to me. I am determined to live a life of wellness, respecting the temple that You have created. I trust that as I seek You, You will guide me in all areas of health and well-being. My life is a testament to Your healing power.

I choose to speak words of health and healing over my body, declaring that I am whole, well, and free from illness. I believe that as I align my words with Your promises, I am inviting Your power to work in me. I am confident that I will experience the fullness of health, living each day with energy and strength. I rejoice in the healing that You have provided, and I trust that my body is continually restored by Your love. My heart is filled with peace, and my life reflects Your healing power.

In Jesus' name, Amen.

24. Hope for the Future

Father, in the name of Jesus, I declare that my heart is filled with hope and expectation for the future You have planned for me. I believe that You hold my future in Your hands, and I trust that it is filled with blessings, opportunities, and purpose. I am grateful for the promises You have spoken over my life, and I choose to look forward with confidence. I know that no matter what challenges may come, my future is secure in You. My heart is lifted, and my spirit is full of hope.

I reject any spirit of fear, doubt, or uncertainty that tries to steal my hope. I refuse to be discouraged by temporary setbacks, knowing that You are working all things for my good. I declare that my hope is anchored in Your faithfulness, unshaken by circumstances. I believe that as I trust in You, I will see the fulfillment of every promise You have made. My hope is strong, grounded in Your love and power.

Thank You, Lord, for the hope that comes from knowing You and believing in Your Word. I am grateful for the vision You have given me, and I trust that every dream and desire You have placed in my heart will come to pass. I believe that my future is bright, filled with opportunities to grow, serve, and experience Your goodness. I am committed to walking in faith, anticipating the great things You have prepared for me. My heart is full of gratitude and hope.

I declare that I am moving forward with boldness and confidence, ready to embrace the future You have designed for me. I am not limited by past experiences or fears but am free to pursue the destiny You have set before me. I trust that as I walk with You, I am continually moving toward the fulfillment of Your plans. I am excited to see what lies ahead, knowing that each step brings me closer to Your promises. My future is filled with hope and purpose.

I choose to speak words of hope and expectation over my life, declaring that I am ready for the good things You have in store. I believe that as I hold on to hope, I am positioning myself to receive all that You have planned. I am confident that my future is secure, and I look forward to each day with joy. I rejoice in the journey, knowing that my hope is in You. My heart is filled with peace, and my life reflects the hope I have in You.

In Jesus' name, Amen.

25. Humility and Servanthood

Father, in the name of Jesus, I declare that I walk in humility and a spirit of servanthood. I know that You resist the proud but give grace to the humble, and I choose to live a life that honors You through humility. I reject any spirit of pride or self-centeredness, choosing instead to see myself and others through Your eyes. I understand that true greatness comes from serving others, and I am committed to using my gifts and talents to lift others up. My heart is set on serving You by serving those around me.

I reject any feelings of entitlement or superiority that try to take root in my heart. I refuse to compare myself to others or seek validation through worldly achievements. I declare that my identity is found in You, and I am content in knowing that I am loved and valued by You. I choose to lift others up, celebrating their successes and supporting them in their journeys. My life is a reflection of Your love and humility.

Thank You, Lord, for the opportunity to serve and to be a blessing to those around me. I am grateful for every chance I have to make a positive impact, no matter how small. I believe that as I humble myself and serve others, You will exalt me in due time. I trust that You see my heart and that You are pleased with my willingness to serve. My joy comes from knowing that I am fulfilling Your call to love and serve others.

I declare that I am sensitive to the needs of those around me, ready to offer help and encouragement. I choose to be a source of strength and comfort, showing compassion and empathy in all my interactions. I believe that as I walk in humility, I am bringing glory to Your name. I am committed to putting others before myself, knowing that You are honored in my actions. My heart is filled with love, and my life is dedicated to serving others.

I choose to speak words of humility and servanthood over my life, declaring that I am here to serve and make a difference. I believe that as I serve with a humble heart, You are working through me to touch lives and bring hope. I am confident that my acts of service are a testimony of Your love and grace. I rejoice in the opportunity to serve, knowing that I am following the example of Christ. My heart is full of joy, and my life reflects the humility of Jesus.

In Jesus' name, Amen.

26. Integrity in Actions and Words

Father, in the name of Jesus, I declare that my life is marked by integrity in everything I do and say. I commit to living a life of honesty, transparency, and truthfulness, knowing that integrity is essential to walking in Your ways. I believe that as I honor You with my actions and words, You will bless and establish my path. I choose to be a person of character, upholding righteousness and honoring You in all things. My heart is set on living a life that reflects Your truth.

I reject any temptation to compromise my values or to act dishonestly. I refuse to allow the world's standards to influence my behavior, choosing instead to live by the principles of Your Word. I declare that I am steadfast in my commitment to integrity, unshaken by external pressures or circumstances. I believe that integrity is a gift that builds trust and strengthens relationships. My life is a testament to Your truth and righteousness.

Thank You, Lord, for the strength and courage to walk in integrity, even when it is difficult. I am grateful for the peace that comes from knowing that my words and actions align with Your will. I believe that as I live with integrity, You are guiding me and blessing my path. I trust that You are using my life as a witness to others, showing them the power of living in truth. My spirit is at peace, and my heart is filled with joy.

I declare that I am mindful of my words and actions, choosing to speak truth and to act with honor. I am committed to being a positive influence, setting an example for others through my integrity. I believe that as I sow seeds of honesty and righteousness, I will reap a harvest of respect and trust. I am determined to walk in truth, knowing that my life is a reflection of Your character. My commitment to integrity is unwavering.

I choose to speak words of integrity over my life, declaring that I am trustworthy and dependable. I believe that as I live in truth, You are establishing my steps and opening doors of opportunity. I am confident that my integrity will bring glory to Your name and be a light to those around me. I rejoice in the peace that comes from a life of honesty and righteousness. My heart is filled with gratitude, and my life reflects Your truth.

In Jesus' name, Amen.

27. Joy in Everyday Life

Father, in the name of Jesus, I declare that my heart is filled with joy, regardless of my circumstances. I believe that true joy comes from knowing You, and I choose to embrace that joy each and every day. I reject any spirit of heaviness or discouragement that tries to weigh me down. I am committed to keeping my focus on Your goodness, allowing Your joy to be my strength. My heart is lifted, and my spirit is full of joy.

I reject any feelings of sadness, frustration, or negativity that try to invade my mind. I refuse to let the challenges of life steal my joy, for I know that my joy is found in You alone. I declare that I am filled with a joy that surpasses understanding, grounded in the assurance of Your love and faithfulness. I believe that as I focus on You, I will experience joy in every season of life. My joy is unshakable, rooted in You.

Thank You, Lord, for the gift of joy that fills my life and sustains me through every situation. I am grateful for the laughter, peace, and contentment that come from knowing You. I believe that as I embrace joy, I am a light to those around me, sharing Your love and hope. I trust that You are using my joy as a testimony to others, showing them the peace that comes from a relationship with You. My spirit is at peace, and my heart is overflowing with joy.

I declare that I choose joy each day, embracing the blessings that You have placed in my life. I am committed to finding reasons to rejoice, to be thankful, and to celebrate the goodness You have shown me. I believe that as I live in joy, I am bringing glory to Your name and reflecting Your love to the world. I am determined to be a source of encouragement, lifting others up through my joy. My life is a testimony of Your joy and peace.

I choose to speak words of joy and gratitude over my life, declaring that my days are filled with laughter and light. I believe that as I keep my eyes on You, I will find joy in the simplest of moments. I am confident that my joy is contagious, inspiring others to seek the peace and happiness that only You can provide. I rejoice in the joy that is mine in You, knowing that it is a gift that nothing can take away. My heart is full of joy, and my life is a reflection of Your love.

In Jesus' name, Amen.

28. Kindness and Compassion

Father, in the name of Jesus, I declare that my life is marked by kindness and compassion toward everyone I encounter. I believe that as Your child, I am called to show love, understanding, and empathy to those around me. I choose to treat others with respect and to offer a listening ear, a helping hand, and a gentle heart. I am committed to reflecting Your love through acts of kindness and compassion. My heart is open, and my spirit is willing to serve others.

I reject any spirit of impatience, harshness, or indifference that tries to harden my heart. I refuse to be swayed by negativity or to let frustration hinder my ability to love others. I declare that I am filled with a spirit of gentleness and kindness, ready to respond with compassion in every situation. I trust that as I walk in kindness, You are using my life to touch and uplift others. My actions reflect the love You have shown me.

Thank You, Lord, for the opportunity to be a vessel of Your love, offering compassion to those who need it most. I am grateful for every chance to make a positive impact, no matter how small. I believe that as I show kindness, I am planting seeds of hope, peace, and healing in the lives of others. I trust that You are working through me, bringing comfort and joy to those around me. My heart is full of gratitude for the privilege of serving others.

I declare that I am intentional about showing kindness in my words, actions, and attitudes. I choose to be slow to anger and quick to listen, seeking to understand before being understood. I believe that as I embrace compassion, I am honoring You and reflecting Your character. I am committed to being a source of love and encouragement, bringing light to everyone I meet. My life is a testament to the power of kindness and compassion.

I choose to speak words of kindness and gentleness over my life, declaring that I am patient, caring, and compassionate. I believe that as I walk in love, I am spreading Your peace and joy to the world. I am confident that my kindness will create a ripple effect, inspiring others to be more compassionate. I rejoice in the opportunity to make a difference through kindness, knowing that it brings glory to You. My heart is filled with love, and my life is a reflection of Your compassion.

In Jesus' name, Amen.

29. Knowledge of God's Word

Father, in the name of Jesus, I declare that I am growing in knowledge and understanding of Your Word. I believe that as I study the Scriptures, You are revealing truth, wisdom, and insight to me. I am committed to spending time in Your Word daily, letting it transform my mind and strengthen my spirit. I know that Your Word is a lamp to my feet and a light to my path, guiding me in all things. My heart is open, and my mind is eager to learn from You.

I reject any spirit of distraction or complacency that tries to keep me from Your Word. I refuse to be content with surface knowledge; I am determined to go deeper, seeking a richer understanding of Your truth. I declare that I am disciplined and focused, committed to growing in my relationship with You through the study of Scripture. I believe that as I make Your Word a priority, I am building a strong foundation of faith. My spirit is hungry for more of You.

Thank You, Lord, for the wisdom and revelation that comes from Your Word. I am grateful for the privilege of learning from You and for the insights that bring clarity and peace to my life. I believe that as I study the Scriptures, I am equipped with the knowledge I need to live a victorious and purposeful life. I trust that Your Word is shaping my thoughts, aligning my desires with

Your will. My heart is filled with gratitude for the gift of Scripture.

I declare that I am a doer of the Word, not just a hearer. I choose to apply the truths I learn, allowing them to transform my actions and attitudes. I believe that as I live according to Your Word, I am reflecting Your character and bringing glory to Your name. I am committed to being a light in the world, sharing the wisdom and hope that come from knowing You. My life is a testimony of the power of Your Word.

I choose to speak words of knowledge and wisdom over my life, declaring that I am continually growing in my understanding of Scripture. I believe that as I meditate on Your Word, I am gaining insight into Your heart and Your ways. I am confident that the knowledge I gain from Scripture will guide me and protect me in every situation. I rejoice in the journey of learning from You, knowing that it brings me closer to Your heart. My mind is renewed, and my life is transformed by Your Word.

In Jesus' name, Amen.

30. Lasting Peace of Mind

Father, in the name of Jesus, I declare that my mind is filled with lasting peace that comes from You alone. I believe that You are the source of true peace, and I trust in Your presence to calm every worry and fear. I choose to focus on Your promises, allowing them to guard my heart and mind against anxiety and doubt. I am committed to casting all my cares on You, knowing that You care deeply for me. My mind is at rest, and my spirit is calm.

I reject any thoughts of worry, stress, or confusion that try to disrupt my peace. I refuse to entertain negative thoughts or to let circumstances steal the peace You have given me. I declare that my mind is set on things above, grounded in the knowledge of Your love and faithfulness. I believe that as I keep my eyes on You, I am surrounded by a peace that surpasses all understanding. My heart is steady, and my mind is unwavering.

Thank You, Lord, for the gift of peace that sustains me in every season of life. I am grateful for the calm assurance that comes from knowing I am safe in Your hands. I believe that as I rest in Your presence, I am free from worry and fear. I trust that You are in control, working all things for my good. My spirit is at peace, and my heart is filled with gratitude.

I declare that I am proactive in maintaining my peace, choosing to pray and seek You in times of trouble. I am committed to protecting my mind from negativity, filling it instead with thoughts of hope, love, and joy. I believe that as I nurture a mindset of peace, I am building resilience and strength. I am determined to live in the peace that only You can provide. My life is a testimony of the power of Your peace.

I choose to speak words of peace and calm over my life, declaring that I am free from stress and anxiety. I believe that as I trust in You, I am experiencing a deep and lasting peace that transcends circumstances. I am confident that Your peace will guard my heart and mind, no matter what I face. I rejoice in the tranquility that fills my life, knowing that it is a gift from You. My heart is light, and my mind is at peace.

In Jesus' name, Amen.

31. Love for God and Others

Father, in the name of Jesus, I declare that my heart is filled with love for You and for others. I believe that You have called me to love, and I am committed to showing compassion, kindness, and understanding to everyone I meet. I choose to let Your love flow through me, reaching those who need encouragement and hope. I know that as I love others, I am fulfilling Your command and bringing glory to Your name. My heart is open, and my spirit is eager to love deeply.

I reject any spirit of hatred, bitterness, or resentment that tries to take root in my heart. I refuse to hold on to unforgiveness or grudges, choosing instead to release every hurt and to love freely. I declare that I am filled with a love that transcends human understanding, a love that is patient, kind, and without conditions. I believe that as I walk in love, I am a reflection of Your heart and character. My life is a testimony of Your love.

Thank You, Lord, for the love You have shown me, a love that is unwavering and unconditional. I am grateful for the way You have transformed my heart, allowing me to love others as You love me. I believe that as I continue to grow in love, I will see relationships flourish and healing take place. I trust that You are using my life to spread Your love to a world that needs it. My spirit is filled with gratitude for the gift of love.

I declare that I am intentional about loving others, even those who may be difficult to love. I choose to see people through Your eyes, recognizing their worth and value as Your creation. I believe that as I show love to others, I am bringing them closer to You. I am committed to being a source of encouragement and support, a vessel of Your love in every interaction. My heart is set on loving others as You have loved me.

I choose to speak words of love and kindness over my life, declaring that I am a person of compassion and empathy. I believe that as I walk in love, I am making a positive impact on the world around me. I am confident that my love for others will bring healing, joy, and peace to their lives. I rejoice in the opportunity to be a beacon of Your love, knowing that it brings glory to You. My heart is full, and my life reflects Your love.

In Jesus' name, Amen.

32. Mindset of Victory

Father, in the name of Jesus, I declare that I have a mindset of victory, rooted in the knowledge that I am more than a conqueror through You. I believe that no challenge is too great, no obstacle too large, because You have already won the victory on my behalf. I choose to walk in confidence, knowing that I am empowered by Your strength and wisdom. I refuse to be defeated or discouraged, for I know that I am victorious in every situation. My mind is set on victory, and my spirit is strong.

I reject any thoughts of defeat, failure, or hopelessness that try to enter my mind. I refuse to entertain negativity or to let fear take root in my heart. I declare that my thoughts are focused on the promises of victory You have given me, and I am unshaken by circumstances. I believe that as I keep my mind on You, I am strengthened and equipped to overcome every challenge. My confidence is in You, my source of victory.

Thank You, Lord, for the victory You have secured for me through Jesus. I am grateful for the assurance that no matter what I face, I am not alone, and I am not defeated. I believe that as I walk in faith, You are guiding me to triumph and success. I trust that You are working all things for my good, turning every situation into a testimony of Your power. My heart is filled with gratitude, and my mind is set on victory.

I declare that I am a warrior in faith, unafraid to face any challenge because I know that You are with me. I choose to approach every situation with a positive mindset, seeing opportunities where others see obstacles. I believe that as I maintain a victorious attitude, I am influencing those around me and glorifying Your name. I am committed to walking in victory, unshaken by trials or setbacks. My life is a reflection of Your triumph.

I choose to speak words of victory and strength over my life, declaring that I am victorious in every area. I believe that as I stand on Your promises, I am moving from glory to glory, from strength to strength. I am confident that my mindset of victory will lead me to success and fulfillment in all things. I rejoice in the victory that is mine in You, knowing that nothing can separate me from Your love. My heart is filled with hope, and my life is a testament to Your power.

In Jesus' name, Amen.

33. New Beginnings and Fresh Starts

Father, in the name of Jesus, I declare that I am stepping into new beginnings and fresh starts, embracing the opportunities You have prepared for me. I believe that You are doing a new thing in my life, opening doors that lead to growth, healing, and purpose. I choose to let go of the past and to move forward with confidence, knowing that my future is in Your hands. I am excited about the new season You are leading me into, trusting that it is filled with blessings and favor. My heart is open, and my spirit is ready for all that is to come.

I reject any feelings of regret, disappointment, or fear that try to hold me back from experiencing new beginnings. I refuse to be chained to the past, for I know that You have given me freedom and hope for the future. I declare that I am filled with anticipation for what lies ahead, unafraid to take bold steps toward my dreams. I trust that You are guiding me into a season of renewal and restoration. My heart is free, and my mind is set on the possibilities before me.

Thank You, Lord, for the gift of new beginnings, for the chance to start afresh and to pursue new goals. I am grateful for Your grace, which allows me to release the past and embrace the future with hope. I believe that as I move forward, You are walking with me, preparing the way for success and fulfillment. I trust that every step I take is leading me closer to the purpose You have designed for me. My spirit is at peace, and my heart is filled with joy.

I declare that I am moving forward with courage, ready to embrace new experiences and opportunities. I choose to be open to change, allowing You to shape my path and to bring new growth into my life. I believe that as I step into this season of fresh starts, You are transforming me from the inside out. I am committed to growing, learning, and becoming all that You have called me to be. My life is a reflection of Your renewing power.

I choose to speak words of hope and expectation over my life, declaring that I am ready for the new things You have in store. I believe that as I embrace change, I am positioning myself to receive Your blessings. I am confident that my future is bright, filled with purpose and joy. I rejoice in the journey of new beginnings, knowing that each day is a gift from You. My heart is filled with hope, and my life is a testament to Your faithfulness.

In Jesus' name, Amen.

34. Obedience to God's Call

Father, in the name of Jesus, I declare that I am committed to walking in obedience to Your call on my life. I believe that You have a unique purpose for me, and I am dedicated to fulfilling it with all my heart. I choose to surrender my plans and desires, aligning myself with Your will and direction. I trust that as I obey, You are leading me into blessings, growth, and divine purpose. My heart is open, and my spirit is willing to follow wherever You lead.

I reject any spirit of hesitation, fear, or rebellion that tries to keep me from fully obeying You. I refuse to let doubt or uncertainty prevent me from taking bold steps in faith. I declare that I am steadfast and resolute, ready to follow Your instructions, no matter the cost. I believe that obedience brings me closer to You and opens the door to a life of fulfillment. My commitment to Your call is unwavering.

Thank You, Lord, for guiding me and giving me the courage to walk in obedience. I am grateful for the assurance that You are with me, empowering me to fulfill Your purpose. I believe that as I obey, You are strengthening me, equipping me, and preparing me for every good work. I trust that You are using my obedience to impact lives and bring glory to Your name. My heart is filled with gratitude for the privilege of serving You.

I declare that I am attentive to Your voice, quick to listen, and eager to follow Your guidance. I am committed to seeking You in all things, allowing Your Word to direct my steps and shape my actions. I believe that as I walk in obedience, I am fulfilling the purpose You have created me for. I am dedicated to being a faithful servant, honoring You in every decision I make. My life is a reflection of my devotion to You.

I choose to speak words of obedience and trust over my life, declaring that I am ready to fulfill the call You have placed on me. I believe that as I obey, I am sowing seeds of faith that will bear fruit for generations. I am confident that my obedience will lead to blessings, purpose, and joy beyond my imagination. I rejoice in the opportunity to serve You, knowing that my life is in Your hands. My heart is full, and my life is surrendered to Your will.

In Jesus' name, Amen.

35. Open Doors of Opportunity

Father, in the name of Jesus, I declare that You are opening doors of opportunity for me, leading me into a season of growth and advancement. I believe that You have prepared good things for me, and I am ready to step into every opportunity You bring. I choose to walk in faith, trusting that You are guiding my steps and opening doors that no one can shut. I am excited about the future, confident that You are leading me to fulfill my purpose. My heart is full of expectation, and my spirit is ready to seize every opportunity.

I reject any feelings of doubt, fear, or limitation that try to hold me back from pursuing new opportunities. I refuse to let past experiences or insecurities hinder my progress. I declare that I am empowered by Your Spirit, equipped to take bold steps and embrace the opportunities before me. I believe that You are positioning me in the right places, connecting me with the right people, and aligning circumstances for my success. My confidence is in You, the One who opens doors.

Thank You, Lord, for the doors You are opening and for the favor You have placed upon my life. I am grateful for the blessings that come from walking in alignment with Your will. I believe that as I pursue these opportunities, You will provide everything I need to succeed. I trust that You are leading me into a season of increase, growth, and fulfillment. My spirit is filled with gratitude and anticipation.

I declare that I am alert and discerning, recognizing every opportunity that comes my way. I choose to seek Your guidance, trusting that You will direct me to the right paths and the right doors. I believe that as I stay connected to You, I am equipped to make wise decisions and to walk boldly into new possibilities. I am committed to honoring You in every opportunity, using my gifts and talents for Your glory. My life is a testimony of Your provision and favor.

I choose to speak words of opportunity and blessing over my life, declaring that doors are opening, and breakthroughs are happening. I believe that as I remain faithful, You are leading me to greater heights and deeper purpose. I am confident that my future is filled with abundance, growth, and impact. I rejoice in the journey, knowing that every opportunity is a gift from You. My heart is full of faith, and my life is a reflection of Your goodness.

In Jesus' name, Amen.

36. Patience in God's Process

Father, in the name of Jesus, I declare that I am patient, trusting in Your process and timing for my life. I believe that You are working behind the scenes, preparing me for the future You have promised. I choose to wait on You with a heart full of hope, confident that every delay serves a purpose. I trust that Your timing is perfect, and I surrender my plans to Your hands. My heart is at peace, and my spirit is patient in Your process.

I reject any spirit of impatience, frustration, or discouragement that tries to overwhelm me. I refuse to let anxiety or fear take root in my heart, for I know that You are in control. I declare that I am steadfast, willing to wait for Your promises, no matter how long it takes. I believe that patience is producing strength, resilience, and faith in me. My focus is on You, and my hope is anchored in Your promises.

Thank You, Lord, for the patience You are developing in me, for the grace to trust Your timing and Your process. I am grateful for the lessons learned in the waiting, for the growth and maturity that come from leaning on You. I believe that as I wait on You, I am being refined and prepared for greater things. I trust that You are using this season to shape me into the person You have called me to be. My spirit is filled with gratitude for Your guidance.

I declare that I am committed to embracing the journey, knowing that every season serves a purpose. I choose to walk in faith, allowing patience to work in me and produce a harvest of blessings. I believe that as I trust in Your process, I am becoming stronger, wiser, and more grounded in my faith. I am determined to wait on You, confident that Your timing is worth the wait. My heart is full of peace, and my life is a reflection of Your faithfulness.

I choose to speak words of patience and trust over my life, declaring that I am aligned with Your perfect timing. I believe that as I wait on You, I am growing closer to You, experiencing peace and joy in the journey. I am confident that my patience will lead to a season of harvest and fulfillment. I rejoice in the process, knowing that Your timing is perfect and Your promises are sure. My heart is anchored in faith, and my life reflects my trust in You.

In Jesus' name, Amen.

37. Perseverance through Challenges

Father, in the name of Jesus, I declare that I am filled with perseverance to overcome any challenge I may face. I believe that You are my strength and my shield, empowering me to stand firm in the face of adversity. I trust that You are with me, guiding me through every difficulty and turning challenges into opportunities for growth. I am committed to pushing forward, never giving up, knowing that I am more than a conqueror in You. My heart is set on victory, and my spirit is unyielding.

I reject any thoughts of defeat, discouragement, or fear that try to invade my mind. I refuse to let obstacles or setbacks weaken my resolve or cause me to doubt Your power in my life. I declare that I am unwavering in my faith, standing strong in the promises You have given me. I believe that every challenge is an opportunity to grow closer to You and to strengthen my character. My confidence is in You, and I am determined to persevere.

Thank You, Lord, for the resilience and endurance You have placed within me. I am grateful for the courage You give me to keep going, even when the journey is difficult. I believe that as I persevere, You are working all things together for my good, bringing me closer to the future You have planned for me. I trust that You are refining me through every challenge, preparing me for greater blessings. My spirit is filled with gratitude, knowing that I am never alone.

I declare that I am tenacious and resilient, unafraid to face any difficulty that comes my way. I choose to rise above discouragement, keeping my eyes fixed on You and moving forward in faith. I believe that as I persevere, I am growing stronger, wiser, and more equipped to fulfill my purpose. I am committed to walking in victory, knowing that You are by my side. My life is a testimony of strength and determination.

I choose to speak words of strength and perseverance over my life, declaring that I am able to overcome every challenge. I believe that as I press on, I am paving the way for blessings and breakthroughs. I am confident that my perseverance will lead me to success and fulfillment in all things. I rejoice in the strength You have given me, knowing that I can do all things through Christ who strengthens me. My heart is full of courage, and my life is a reflection of Your power.

In Jesus' name, Amen.

38. Protection from Harm

Father, in the name of Jesus, I declare that I am surrounded by Your divine protection in every area of my life. I trust that You are my refuge and fortress, guarding me from all harm and shielding me from every attack of the enemy. I believe that no weapon formed against me shall prosper, for I am covered by the blood of Jesus. I am confident in Your promises of safety and protection, knowing that You watch over me at all times. My heart is at peace, and my spirit is secure.

I reject any spirit of fear, anxiety, or worry that tries to take hold of my mind. I refuse to let the uncertainties of life steal my peace, for I know that I am safe in Your hands. I declare that I am protected from all forms of harm, danger, and evil. I believe that You have placed angels around me, guarding and guiding me in all my ways. My trust is in You, my protector and deliverer.

Thank You, Lord, for the assurance of Your protection, for the peace that comes from knowing I am safe in Your care. I am grateful for the covering of Your presence, which shields me from harm and keeps me secure. I believe that as I walk in faith, You are keeping me safe from every threat, seen and unseen. I trust that You are a faithful guardian, watching over me and my loved ones. My heart is filled with gratitude for Your constant protection.

I declare that I walk with confidence, knowing that I am protected by Your mighty hand. I choose to live without fear, embracing each day with peace and assurance. I believe that as I rest in Your protection, I am free to live boldly and pursue my purpose. I am committed to trusting You fully, knowing that You are my defender and shield. My life is a testimony of Your protection and love.

I choose to speak words of safety and peace over my life, declaring that I am secure under Your covering. I believe that as I place my trust in You, no harm shall come near me or my household. I am confident that Your protection surrounds me like a shield, keeping me safe from all danger. I rejoice in the peace that comes from knowing You are always with me. My heart is at rest, and my life reflects the security I have in You.

In Jesus' name, Amen.

39. Provision for Every Need

Father, in the name of Jesus, I declare that You are my provider, and I trust that You will meet every need in my life. I believe that You are faithful to supply all my needs according to Your riches in glory. I am confident that You see every detail of my life, and You are orchestrating provision in ways I may not even see. I am grateful for the resources You have given me and the blessings You continue to provide. My heart is at peace, knowing that I am cared for by You.

I reject any spirit of lack, worry, or fear regarding my needs. I refuse to let financial concerns or uncertainty consume my thoughts, for I know that You are my source. I declare that I lack nothing, for You are my shepherd, guiding me and providing all that I need. I trust that as I seek You first, everything else will be added to me. My focus is on You, and my faith is in Your provision.

Thank You, Lord, for the abundance You have promised to Your children. I am grateful for Your generosity and for the ways You bless me, both seen and unseen. I believe that as I walk in faith and obedience, You will open doors of opportunity and increase. I trust that You are arranging divine provision for every aspect of my life. My spirit is filled with gratitude for Your unwavering faithfulness.

I declare that I am a wise steward of the resources You have given me, using them to honor You and to bless others. I am committed to living with a heart of generosity, trusting that as I give, You will continue to provide. I believe that as I manage my resources faithfully, You will multiply them and supply even more. I am dedicated to using my blessings to serve and uplift those around me. My life is a reflection of Your abundant provision.

I choose to speak words of abundance and faith over my life, declaring that every need is met in Jesus' name. I believe that as I trust in You, You will provide more than enough for every situation. I am confident that Your provision is constant and unfailing, allowing me to live without fear of lack. I rejoice in the knowledge that You are my provider, and I am blessed beyond measure. My heart is filled with peace, and my life reflects Your provision.

In Jesus' name, Amen.

40. Purposeful Living Daily

Father, in the name of Jesus, I declare that I am living each day with purpose, intentionality, and focus on what truly matters. I believe that You have created me with a unique purpose, and I am committed to pursuing it with my whole heart. I choose to start each day with a sense of direction, knowing that every step I take brings me closer to fulfilling Your plans for me. I am determined to live a life that reflects Your love and serves others. My heart is set on making each day count for Your glory.

I reject any spirit of aimlessness, distraction, or complacency that tries to steal my focus. I refuse to let the busyness of life keep me from pursuing what truly matters. I declare that I am disciplined, organized, and motivated, using my time and talents wisely. I believe that as I walk in purpose, I am empowered by Your Spirit to make a difference. My life is centered on You, and my actions are aligned with Your will.

Thank You, Lord, for the purpose You have given me and for guiding me every step of the way. I am grateful for the direction and vision You have placed in my heart, helping me to live with intentionality. I believe that as I seek You daily, You are revealing new opportunities and opening doors to fulfill my purpose. I trust that You are using me to impact lives and bring hope to others. My spirit is filled with gratitude for the life You have designed for me.

I declare that I am focused on what matters, refusing to be distracted by things that don't align with my purpose. I choose to prioritize my time, energy, and resources on activities that bring me closer to fulfilling Your call. I believe that as I live each day with intention, I am creating a life of significance and impact. I am committed to being a faithful steward of every opportunity You place before me. My heart is dedicated to purposeful living.

I choose to speak words of purpose and direction over my life, declaring that I am equipped and empowered to fulfill Your plans. I believe that as I walk in purpose, I am living a life that is rich in meaning and filled with joy. I am confident that my days are purposeful, meaningful, and a testimony of Your guidance. I rejoice in the journey, knowing that each day brings me closer to my destiny. My heart is full of peace, and my life is a reflection of Your purpose.

In Jesus' name, Amen.

41. Renewed Strength and Energy

Father, in the name of Jesus, I declare that I am filled with renewed strength and energy to face each day. I believe that You are the source of my strength, refreshing me physically, mentally, and spiritually. I choose to trust in You to renew my energy and give me the endurance I need to accomplish everything You have set before me. I am confident that as I rest in Your presence, You are restoring my strength like the eagle's. My heart is lifted, and my spirit is energized.

I reject any feelings of exhaustion, weariness, or burnout that try to drain my energy. I refuse to let fatigue or stress control my life, knowing that I am empowered by Your Spirit. I declare that I am rejuvenated and revitalized, able to face every task with enthusiasm and joy. I believe that as I rely on You, I am strengthened from within and able to persevere. My confidence is in You, my source of strength and renewal.

Thank You, Lord, for the gift of renewed energy and for the strength to accomplish my daily tasks. I am grateful for Your presence, which brings me peace and refreshes my spirit. I believe that as I prioritize time with You, I am continually refilled and recharged. I trust that You are giving me the stamina I need to fulfill my purpose. My heart is filled with gratitude for the vitality that comes from knowing You.

I declare that I am diligent in taking care of my body, mind, and spirit, nurturing the strength You have given me. I choose to be intentional about rest, exercise, and time with You, honoring the temple You have entrusted to me. I believe that as I make healthy choices, I am building resilience and energy for the days ahead. I am committed to living a balanced life, fully equipped to serve You and others. My life is a testimony of health and vitality.

I choose to speak words of strength and energy over my life, declaring that I am empowered to accomplish all that You have called me to do. I believe that as I draw strength from You, I am equipped for every challenge and ready for every opportunity. I am confident that my renewed energy is a gift from You, enabling me to make a positive impact. I rejoice in the vitality You provide, knowing that I am refreshed and strengthened daily. My heart is full, and my life reflects Your strength.

In Jesus' name, Amen.

42. Restoration of Broken Relationships

Father, in the name of Jesus, I declare that You are restoring every broken relationship in my life, bringing healing, understanding, and unity. I believe that You are a God of reconciliation, and I trust in Your power to mend hearts and repair what has been damaged. I am committed to being a vessel of forgiveness and love, open to reconciliation and healing. I choose to release any resentment or bitterness, allowing Your peace to fill my heart. My spirit is ready for restoration, and my heart is open to Your healing touch.

I reject any spirit of division, anger, or pride that tries to hinder reconciliation. I refuse to let past hurts or misunderstandings keep me from experiencing peace and unity in my relationships. I declare that I am willing to forgive and to seek forgiveness, creating a foundation for healing and restoration. I believe that as I open my heart to You, You are guiding me toward healthy, restored connections. My relationships are rooted in Your love and grace.

Thank You, Lord, for the work You are doing to restore relationships in my life. I am grateful for the healing and unity that only You can bring. I believe that as I surrender my relationships to You, You are creating bonds that are stronger and more resilient than before. I trust that You are using every experience, even the painful ones, to bring growth and closeness. My heart is filled with gratitude for the gift of restored relationships.

I declare that I am patient and understanding, willing to listen and to communicate with compassion. I choose to be a source of encouragement and peace, building up those around me rather than tearing down. I believe that as I show kindness and empathy, I am fostering relationships that reflect Your love. I am committed to nurturing healthy connections and to being a source of light in every relationship. My life is a reflection of Your love and unity.

I choose to speak words of healing and reconciliation over my relationships, declaring that they are blessed and restored. I believe that as I trust in You, You are mending every broken bond and renewing every connection. I am confident that my relationships are filled with love, understanding, and mutual respect. I rejoice in the restoration You are bringing, knowing that it is a testament to Your power. My heart is full, and my relationships are a reflection of Your healing touch.

In Jesus' name, Amen.

43. Self-Control in All Situations

Father, in the name of Jesus, I declare that I am filled with self-control, able to remain steady and disciplined in all situations. I believe that You have given me the power to control my thoughts, actions, and emotions, allowing me to live a life that honors You. I choose to walk in self-control, letting Your Spirit guide me in every decision and response. I am committed to exercising restraint, patience, and wisdom, no matter what I face. My heart is grounded, and my mind is focused on living a life of balance and integrity.

I reject any impulses, temptations, or distractions that try to sway me from walking in self-control. I refuse to be influenced by negative emotions or pressures, knowing that I am empowered by Your Spirit to rise above. I declare that I am strong, resilient, and able to respond with wisdom and grace in every circumstance. I believe that as I exercise self-control, I am growing in character and aligning myself with Your will. My confidence is in You, and my actions are a reflection of Your strength.

Thank You, Lord, for the gift of self-control and for the peace that comes from knowing I can trust in You. I am grateful for Your guidance, which helps me remain disciplined and focused on what truly matters. I believe that as I lean on You, I am empowered to make choices that lead to peace and fulfillment. I trust that You are helping me grow in self-discipline, shaping me to reflect

Your character. My heart is filled with gratitude for the strength You provide.

I declare that I am intentional about my words, thoughts, and actions, choosing to honor You in all things. I am committed to maintaining a calm spirit, even in challenging situations, showing patience and understanding. I believe that as I practice self-control, I am creating a life of stability, integrity, and peace. I am determined to be a source of encouragement and a light to others, living with purpose and conviction. My life is a reflection of the discipline and balance You have instilled in me.

I choose to speak words of self-control and discipline over my life, declaring that I am steady, focused, and unwavering in my commitment to You. I believe that as I walk in self-control, I am setting an example for others and bringing glory to Your name. I am confident that my strength and self-discipline will lead to success and fulfillment in every area. I rejoice in the peace and order that self-control brings, knowing that it is a gift from You. My heart is full, and my life is a reflection of Your wisdom.

In Jesus' name, Amen.

44. Spiritual Discernment and Wisdom

Father, in the name of Jesus, I declare that I am filled with spiritual discernment and wisdom, able to understand and make decisions that align with Your will. I believe that You are guiding me with clarity and insight, helping me to see beyond appearances and understand the heart of every matter. I choose to seek Your wisdom in all things, knowing that You provide the insight I need to navigate life with confidence. I am committed to following Your Spirit, allowing Your discernment to lead me. My heart is open, and my mind is receptive to Your guidance.

I reject any spirit of confusion, doubt, or indecision that tries to cloud my judgment. I refuse to let fear or uncertainty keep me from making wise, God-honoring choices. I declare that I am clear-minded, focused, and sensitive to Your Spirit's leading. I believe that as I seek Your wisdom, I am equipped with understanding that surpasses human knowledge. My confidence is in You, and my decisions are grounded in Your truth.

Thank You, Lord, for the wisdom and discernment You provide, guiding me in every season and situation. I am grateful for the peace that comes from knowing I can rely on You to lead me rightly. I believe that as I meditate on Your Word and seek Your counsel, I am growing in spiritual understanding. I trust that You are revealing truth to me, helping me to discern what is best and to follow Your perfect path. My heart is filled with gratitude for Your constant guidance.

I declare that I am attentive to Your voice, sensitive to Your Spirit, and ready to act on the wisdom You provide. I choose to be cautious, thoughtful, and discerning in every decision I make. I believe that as I walk in discernment, I am a light to others, showing them the way to truth and peace. I am committed to being a faithful steward of the wisdom You have entrusted to me, using it to glorify You. My life is a reflection of Your wisdom and insight.

I choose to speak words of wisdom and discernment over my life, declaring that I am guided, protected, and enlightened by Your Spirit. I believe that as I seek Your counsel, I am equipped with understanding and insight beyond my natural ability. I am confident that my life is filled with clarity and purpose, as I rely on Your wisdom daily. I rejoice in the peace that discernment brings, knowing that I am on the path You have set for me. My heart is at peace, and my life reflects Your guidance.

In Jesus' name, Amen.

45. Steadfast Faith in Uncertain Times

Father, in the name of Jesus, I declare that I have steadfast faith, anchored in You, even in uncertain times. I believe that You are my rock and my refuge, unchanging and faithful, no matter what is happening around me. I choose to hold on to Your promises, trusting that You are with me and will guide me through every challenge. I am committed to keeping my eyes on You, knowing that my faith is strengthened in times of testing. My heart is steady, and my spirit is filled with unwavering faith.

I reject any spirit of fear, doubt, or anxiety that tries to shake my confidence in You. I refuse to let circumstances dictate my faith, choosing instead to trust in Your power and sovereignty. I declare that my faith is strong, rooted in Your Word, and unshaken by the uncertainties of life. I believe that as I walk in faith, You are carrying me through every trial and bringing me to victory. My trust is in You, my faithful provider and protector.

Thank You, Lord, for the peace and assurance that come from knowing You are with me, even in difficult seasons. I am grateful for Your promises that remind me of Your love and faithfulness. I believe that as I keep my heart fixed on You, I am experiencing peace and joy, regardless of what is happening around me. I trust that You are using every challenge to strengthen my faith and draw me closer to You. My heart is filled with gratitude for Your unchanging presence.

I declare that I am steadfast and resilient, able to face uncertainty with courage and confidence. I choose to keep my focus on You, letting Your Word be my anchor and my guide. I believe that as I remain steadfast, I am growing in faith, hope, and endurance. I am committed to walking in peace, knowing that my faith is not dependent on my circumstances. My life is a testimony of unwavering faith in a faithful God.

I choose to speak words of faith and hope over my life, declaring that I am anchored in You, unshaken by any storm. I believe that as I trust in You, I am filled with courage, strength, and peace that surpasses all understanding. I am confident that my faith will lead me to victory, as I hold on to Your promises. I rejoice in the assurance that You are my refuge and strength, a very present help in times of trouble. My heart is at peace, and my life reflects my steadfast faith in You.

In Jesus' name, Amen.

46. Strength to Resist Temptation

Father, in the name of Jesus, I declare that I have the strength and power to resist every temptation that comes my way. I believe that You are faithful and provide a way of escape in every moment of trial. I choose to stand firm in my faith, knowing that I am empowered by Your Spirit to overcome every temptation. I am committed to living a life that honors You, rejecting anything that would pull me away from Your will. My heart is steadfast, and my spirit is determined to walk in purity.

I reject any desire, thought, or habit that does not align with Your Word. I refuse to let temptation have power over me, for I am free in Christ and empowered to choose righteousness. I declare that I am filled with the Spirit, able to discern right from wrong and to resist anything that would harm my relationship with You. I believe that as I walk in obedience, I am protected and strengthened by Your presence. My confidence is in You, and I am victorious over temptation.

Thank You, Lord, for the strength You give me to resist temptation and for the wisdom to make choices that lead to life. I am grateful for Your guidance, which helps me to recognize and avoid anything that could pull me away from You. I believe that as I seek Your will, You are transforming my desires and aligning my heart with Yours. I trust that You are renewing my mind, helping me to focus on what is pure, true, and pleasing to You. My heart is filled with gratitude for the freedom I have in You.

I declare that I am vigilant and alert, guarding my mind and heart against anything that would lead me astray. I choose to fill my life with positive influences, seeking Your guidance in every choice I make. I believe that as I stay close to You, I am equipped to resist any temptation that comes my way. I am committed to living a life of purity, integrity, and faithfulness. My life is a reflection of my commitment to You.

I choose to speak words of strength and victory over my life, declaring that I am empowered to overcome every temptation. I believe that as I stand on Your promises, I am free from the grip of sin and able to walk in righteousness. I am confident that my choices honor You and lead me closer to the purpose You have for me. I rejoice in the freedom that comes from walking in obedience to You. My heart is full, and my life reflects Your strength.

In Jesus' name, Amen.

47. Trust in God's Plan

Father, in the name of Jesus, I declare that I trust fully in Your plan for my life, knowing that You have designed it with purpose and love. I believe that Your plans are perfect, even when I may not understand them, and I am committed to following wherever You lead. I choose to surrender my desires and to align my will with Yours, trusting that You know what is best for me. I am confident that You are guiding my steps, working all things for my good. My heart is secure, and my faith is rooted in Your wisdom.

I reject any spirit of worry, doubt, or impatience that tries to shake my confidence in Your plan. I refuse to let uncertainty steal my peace, choosing instead to rest in Your promises. I declare that I am steadfast, trusting that You are in control and that Your timing is perfect. I believe that as I place my trust in You, I am experiencing peace and joy, regardless of my circumstances. My confidence is in You, my faithful provider and guide.

Thank You, Lord, for the assurance that comes from knowing You have a beautiful plan for my life. I am grateful for the peace that fills my heart as I trust in Your direction and purpose. I believe that as I lean on You, You are unfolding a future that is beyond my imagination. I trust that every moment, every season, is part of Your greater purpose for me. My heart is filled with gratitude for the journey You are leading me on.

I declare that I am committed to walking in faith, letting go of control and embracing Your plan with joy. I choose to focus on Your promises rather than on temporary setbacks or delays. I believe that as I trust in You, I am discovering new strength, resilience, and peace. I am dedicated to pursuing Your will, knowing that it leads to fulfillment and joy. My life is a testament to the beauty of trusting in You.

I choose to speak words of faith and trust over my life, declaring that I am surrendered to Your plan and at peace with Your purpose. I believe that as I walk in trust, I am receiving blessings, guidance, and direction from You. I am confident that my future is secure, filled with hope and abundance, as I trust in Your goodness. I rejoice in the assurance that You are leading me, knowing that I am safe in Your hands. My heart is full, and my life reflects my trust in You.

In Jesus' name, Amen.

48. Unity in the Body of Christ

Father, in the name of Jesus, I declare that I am a vessel of unity, promoting peace and love within the Body of Christ. I believe that You have called me to be part of a family of believers, working together to reflect Your love and purpose in the world. I am committed to building bridges, fostering understanding, and celebrating diversity within Your church. I choose to walk in love and to put others before myself, creating an environment of unity and acceptance. My heart is set on seeing the Body of Christ thrive in harmony.

I reject any spirit of division, strife, or jealousy that tries to create discord among believers. I refuse to participate in gossip, negativity, or criticism that harms the unity of the church. I declare that I am an advocate for peace, choosing to see others through Your eyes and to speak words that build up rather than tear down. I believe that as I pursue unity, I am contributing to the strength and health of the Body of Christ. My life is a reflection of Your love and grace.

Thank You, Lord, for the community of believers You have surrounded me with, for the friendships and support that come from being part of Your family. I am grateful for the opportunity to grow, serve, and worship alongside my brothers and sisters in Christ. I believe that as I walk in love and unity, I am honoring You and helping to fulfill Your purpose. I trust that You are using the Body of Christ to bring healing, hope, and salvation to the world. My spirit is filled with gratitude for the blessing of unity.

I declare that I am proactive in promoting unity, seeking to understand others' perspectives and to find common ground. I choose to be quick to forgive, patient in conflict, and gracious in disagreement. I believe that as I walk in unity, I am creating a space where the love of Christ is evident to all. I am committed to being a source of peace and encouragement, helping to build a church that reflects Your heart. My life is dedicated to fostering harmony and togetherness.

I choose to speak words of unity and love over the Body of Christ, declaring that we are one in purpose, mission, and love for You. I believe that as we work together in unity, we are a powerful witness to the world of Your love and truth. I am confident that the church is strong, thriving, and united as we focus on our shared mission. I rejoice in the unity of the Body of Christ, knowing that it is a gift from You. My heart is full, and my life reflects my commitment to unity.

In Jesus' name, Amen.

49. Victory Over Adversity

Father, in the name of Jesus, I declare that I am victorious over every adversity I face, empowered by Your strength to overcome all obstacles. I believe that You have made me more than a conqueror, and I am confident that no challenge is too great for me to overcome. I choose to face adversity with courage, trusting that You are with me, guiding and strengthening me every step of the way. I am committed to walking in faith, knowing that You are working all things together for my good. My heart is filled with hope, and my spirit is strong in Your power.

I reject any thoughts of defeat, despair, or fear that try to take hold of my mind. I refuse to let setbacks or difficulties steal my peace, for I know that I am anchored in You. I declare that I am resilient, unshaken by trials, and confident in Your ability to lead me to victory. I believe that every adversity is an opportunity to grow, to learn, and to draw closer to You. My confidence is in You, my faithful deliverer and shield.

Thank You, Lord, for the strength, courage, and resilience You have placed within me. I am grateful for the assurance that no matter what I face, I am not alone, and I am equipped to overcome. I believe that as I trust in You, I am moving from strength to strength and from victory to victory. I trust that You are using every challenge to refine me and to bring glory to Your name.

My heart is filled with gratitude for the victories You have already won on my behalf.

I declare that I am steadfast and unmovable, choosing to press forward in faith regardless of my circumstances. I choose to keep my eyes on You, confident that You are leading me to triumph in every situation. I believe that as I walk in victory, I am a light to others, showing them the power of faith in You. I am determined to live boldly, facing every challenge with strength and conviction. My life is a reflection of Your power and victory.

I choose to speak words of victory and strength over my life, declaring that I am triumphant in all things. I believe that as I stand on Your promises, I am empowered to overcome any adversity and to walk in peace and joy. I am confident that my journey is one of victory, filled with testimonies of Your faithfulness and love. I rejoice in the assurance that I am victorious through You, my Savior and King. My heart is full, and my life is a testament to Your triumph.

In Jesus' name, Amen.

50. Wisdom for Life's Choices

Father, in the name of Jesus, I declare that I am filled with wisdom and understanding for every decision I make in life. I believe that You are the source of all wisdom, and I trust You to guide me in every choice, big or small. I choose to seek Your counsel first, knowing that Your ways are higher than mine and that You have a perfect plan for me. I am committed to living a life of discernment, aligning my choices with Your will and purpose. My heart is open, and my mind is receptive to Your wisdom.

I reject any spirit of confusion, impulsiveness, or indecision that tries to cloud my judgment. I refuse to make choices based on fear, pressure, or worldly influences, choosing instead to rely on Your guidance. I declare that I am focused, discerning, and able to recognize the paths that lead to peace and fulfillment. I believe that as I seek Your wisdom, You are illuminating my path and helping me make choices that honor You. My confidence is in You, my wise and faithful guide.

Thank You, Lord, for the wisdom and insight You provide as I navigate the complexities of life. I am grateful for the clarity that comes from Your Spirit, helping me to make decisions that align with Your purpose. I believe that as I grow in wisdom, I am equipped to handle any challenge with grace and understanding. I trust that You are directing my steps, leading me toward success, peace, and purpose. My heart is filled with gratitude for the wisdom You freely give.

I declare that I am patient and deliberate in my choices, taking time to seek Your direction and to weigh every decision carefully. I am committed to being a faithful steward of the opportunities and responsibilities You have given me. I believe that as I walk in wisdom, I am laying a foundation for a life that reflects Your glory. I am determined to make choices that bring honor to You and that fulfill the purpose You have for me. My life is a reflection of Your wisdom and grace.

I choose to speak words of wisdom and clarity over my life, declaring that I am guided by Your Spirit in every decision. I believe that as I trust in Your counsel, I am experiencing peace, confidence, and success in all areas. I am confident that my choices are leading me closer to You and to the life You have planned for me. I rejoice in the knowledge that You are my constant guide, helping me to walk in wisdom every day. My heart is at peace, and my life is a testament to Your wisdom.

In Jesus' name, Amen.

Made in the USA
Columbia, SC
14 December 2024